The Hollowed Edge of Almost

Karen Richards

Copyright © 2024 Karen Richards
All rights reserved. No part of this publication including the cover image may be reproduced, distributed, or transmitted in any form or by any means, without the prior written permission of the publisher.

Front Cover Design by Islam Farid
ISBN: 978-0-6489919-2-2

DEDICATION

I dedicate this book to anyone who has faltered, fallen and lived to learn to fly again

xx

CONTENTS

Falter	7
Fall	65
Fly	121

FALTER

"When it comes to dreams, one may falter, but the only way to fail is to abandon them."

Jonathan Rhys Meyers

fly

this world
slowly plucked
the beautiful wings
from her frail body
then dared ask
"little girl, why is it
you cannot fly?"

one glorious morn'

dawn stretches lazily across sand
saline ebb of waves
gently row morning to shore
playful breeze tosses
the golden orb high into the sky
leaving elongated shadows
to mimic every movement
beneath saffron canopies of the sun
I swim toward the horizon
leave my soft, grey ghost
to wait on the shore
befriending hungry gull
rummaging the tide's buffet
there is peace in my heart
in the weightlessness of silence
and in the glorious arrival of morn'

infant orchestra

my heart is an infant orchestra
which knows only one tune -
the melodic symphony of numbness

martyr

how much longer
must we hurt for this love
cross lonely battlefields
with little hope of peace
before we realise
some wars can't be won
without sacrifice
without a martyr
to throw themselves
at the feet of love

architecture

love targets
the softness in us first
it bends and moulds
the parts we hate most
into everything beautiful

isn't it romantic
to believe for a moment
that something as powerful
as love can make a home
in the flawed architecture
of a heart?

innocent abandon

life was still
back when waist-high thickets
sensed the joy
of our childish laughter
as we ran blindly
and with innocent abandon
into the unknown

these are the memories
that haunt me
how lost we became
as our ages
and innocence outgrew
the lifespan of long
barren pastures

now bare earth barely recalls
how to mimic the stillness
and bare feet forgot long ago
just how to grasp it

mahogany

this mahogany bed frame
holds your silhouette
these sheets
whimpers of ecstasy
these pillows
a lifetime of tears

never have you felt
further away
never have I needed
you more

afterthoughts

I caress this mug
of afterthoughts
foam peaks undulating
with each exhale
ponder sweet promises
sinking granule-like
beneath the white,
billowy clouds
dissolving, disintegrating
while I mull over why life
always tastes sweeter
when I too disappear

exposed

as dawn holds
aloft morning light
a waning moon
gathers stars
wraps them
in billowing cloud
and I am lost
until dusk calls
exposing me
naked, covered only
by darkness

love by name

I knew love by name
but I had never known it
by the smile of someone's eyes
until you

things I haven't quite figured out yet

whether the reason the ocean is blue
is because it bows down at our feet,
yet we never take notice

why people who say they love us,
hurt us

why the words once flowing
with abundance, now rarely trickle

why caterpillars become butterflies
yet we are trapped in broken bodies

why modern medicine
can't cure cancer yet

why I can find
a whole universe in the stars
but I still can't find you

a million lifetimes

our love feels
as though it has existed
a million lifetimes
I wonder if we ever got it right
in any of them

this window

I fell through this window
where cracks of light
illuminate the sway
of freshly cut grass
between lazing blades
where sleeping dandelions
have long ago
put their wishes to bed
there is no sound
but a lone cricket chirping
his rendition of howling
to the midnight moon
which kissed our feet
and I am home
swaddled by a galaxy of stars
broken by the absence of you

little girl

as I pull back the curtains
to greet another day
I find the little girl in me
cowering, pleading
for someone to love her
unconditionally
and each night as I close them
she cries as she watches me
all these years later
on her knees
still praying for the same

abandoned ghost

I am the grown-up reflection
of a girl whose ghost
I abandoned years ago

if people were seasons
after @writtenbyshannon

if people were seasons
then I long to be spring
to push myself
through sodden earth
to not let my face
be concealed by shadows
I have learned to exist in
I long to be the softness
of green grass between toes
the kind people fall in love with
so much they want to stay

if people were seasons
then I could never be summer
longed for; welcomed
with bronzed arms and icecream hearts
I could never be the line between
cool water and burning sand
because I am all or nothing
I could never be a smile
a beach sunset, a receding tide
because they all return
when all I ever am is a memory

if people were seasons
then I am the fall
a plethora of cries
wailing between winds of agony
I am leaves; crumpled
amber stains upon the skin
where you held me down
against my will
my throat, still bears the scars

if people were seasons
then I am winter
a season of loneliness
left with frost bitten fingers
and an ice cold heart
desperate for warmth
but unable to feel
I am gumboots left out in the snow
a warm jacket riddled with holes
where life seeps out
and winter makes a home

I am a season
which was never taught
to hold itself with love

names I have called myself

I am a misfit
a jigsaw puzzle with the missing corners
I have spent decades
tearing apart everything good
trying to find,
just to feel complete

I am blank pages of a journal
someone gifted me once
too afraid to muddy
their alabaster perfection
with messy thoughts
instead filed away out of reach,
on shelves with bookends
of procrastination and hope

I am the colour purple
contusions in various shades
proudly displayed
an emoji heart to show love
the sweet aroma
of lilac-tinged irises in spring
the grape-flavoured bubble gum
I loved as a child

I am flawed
in the most beautiful ways
a petal, bent from leaning
too far towards the sun
a frosted piece of beach glass
with a thousand stories to tell
a scratched record
stuck in the groove,
in the groove,
in the groove
of a favourite song

and I am a broken heart
risking everything,
all in the name of love

never felt lonelier

you tease from my skin
the emptiness I carry
and make it whole

coax from my lips
words I tell myself
I will never say again

what I really mean to say is
I've never felt lonelier
than I am when I'm with you

temporary heart

I am a temporary heart
of little use
once bled dry
to fill your own
tossed aside
amid the ruins
of those who give
just a little too much
of what little love
they keep
tucked away
in their temporary hearts

wicked tongue

she trusted too much
the way his eyes danced
ignored his wicked tongue
and devilish grin
painted to kissable lips
which would one day
bring her to her knees

stepping stone

I live my life
as a stepping stone
the conduit
between hurt
and happiness
a hop and a skip
on the way
to a destination
but never enough
for anyone
to want to stay

the word love

we bounced the word love
back and forth
back and forth
until its very meaning
became cold, frigid,
frozen in bubbles
of suspended animation
not more than a syllable
we believed we should feel
but never truly did

you broke me softly

you broke me softly
tore me to pieces
like freshly baked bread
on a cold winter day
with the want and hunger
of gentle fingertips

you broke me softly
handfuls of forget-me-not petals
disembodied from their stem
a childhood game
of he loves me, he loves me not

you broke me softly
your words; a pocket book thesaurus
discovering new and unfamiliar ways
to tell me you loved me
without ever loving me at all

rummage the stars

I rummage the stars
searching for you
fingertips burning
blind to the truth
that eventually
everything will fade
into nothingness
even you

mockery of misery

I have a heart
which makes
a mockery
of misery
and creates art
with the remnants
of love

the thing about love

that's the thing about love
it roars like an ocean
or leaves like the tide

braille

I will never allow
your fingertips
to treat my skin
as braille
blind to everything
but your touch

sonnets of spring

you exhale sonnets of spring
pollination of our fingers
a honey bee's hum
and nectar-laden stems
nestle into fertile soil

on yonder
the bluest of lilies
fade beneath strands
of afternoon sun
craving that which
is forever fleeting

and somewhere
beyond undulating hills
the sun dies
leaving us to ponder
why glimpses of heaven
never last

clenched teeth

I have held these words
like a final breath
between my ribs
like chaos
behind clenched teeth
but words escape me now
I don't have the strength
to love you anymore

summer

do you notice
how summer
swallows the
existence of spring
inhaling life
and leaving
the charred corpse
of a season
in its wake

you, you are
summer incarnate
and I yearn to be
anything but spring

relic

I am a museum
a colosseum
a lost and found
of memories and moments
you are just another relic
displayed to the world
but never meant
for me

solitary syllable

we hesitate somewhere
between echoes and whispers
abandoned in a valley

where love is a solitary syllable
left lingering in the minuscule space
between almost touching fingertips

waiting for us
to surrender ourselves
to the sound

crimson

a blush of crimson
radiates across cheeks
as your playful, wanton
sighs echo the canyon
of my thighs
in my head
what sounds like
subtle moans
roar like thunder
from beneath my ribs
as I long for a happier ending
than this long-forgotten
memory of you

quiet ache

I wear a quiet ache
nestled against
my collarbone
where whispered
'I love you's'
came to rest
and stayed
long after
you left

redemption

dawn always arrives with hope
blush softness of pink calla lily
erupting into dust on the horizon
ashes of yesterday reincarnate,
reborn, returned
as the gift of redemption
to lost souls

ruminations

you were once
something
now nothing more
than ruminations
scratched into paper
and set alight
to cradle me
with warmth
in this cold
and empty bed

worth the misery

you tell me I am
worth the misery
and I reply
you are no longer
worth the ache

my therapist told me

my therapist told me
to honour my feelings
to give them the voice
they've never had
and those who love me
will stay ....

bruised

my hands are bruised
tired of fighting
to be part of places
I have never belonged

warheads overhead

I found safety
in silence
until it found me
standing accused
at the guillotine
hoarse, pressed
against the
chopping block
of activism
there is no safety
no shelter, no freedom
just the roar
of warheads overhead
peace will never be
ours again

witness hope

if you could just see past
this relentless darkness
you would witness hope
surging my bloodstream
why else would I spend
a lifetime waiting for you?

more than a scar

there is a little part of me
which doesn't want
the wounds of you to heal
because what more
will we ever be
than a scar

dear august

we find each other,
again in the depth of despair,
hollow heart emptied of love,
mind full of regrets.
I wonder if it is the season,
the chilled winter breath
which pulls love to warmer climates
or if it is me and my cemetery heart dragging these
ice cold bones
which drives them away.
I guess we will never know.
I am beginning to wonder though,
if I am a season all of my own,
one people can't wait to escape.

too emotional

he tells me I'm too emotional
so I choke back the tears
and openly accept the knife
being driven between my ribs
disguise the sob which threatens
to escape, with laughter
I guess behind the armour
I'm always going to be
just a little too damaged to be loved

doormat

so what if I confuse
loneliness for unworthiness
you confuse my heart
for a doormat
isn't it basically
the same thing?

bear burden

I am yet to master
the art of letting go
instead, I bear the burden
of every mistake
every poorly thought out
apology which never
left these lips
imagine all these hands
could embrace if not
for holding on

habitual battle

there is a world of war
inside my head
a habitual battle
between heart and mind
and as with every war
collateral damage follows
I'm sorry you have to be mine

paper moon

I hold life
with the fragility
of a paper moon
knowing even
a solitary tear
could unbalance
the universe
and leave the world
in eternal night

how I really feel about January
after @hergreyside_

the scorching summer sun
stings my eyes
blinds me to all possibilities of hope
it burns your touch from my skin
leaving me bleeding-heart red

it dehydrates my tongue
until it is lifeless
and parched of words
it shows me the true meaning
of loneliness
ice-cream for one
just doesn't satisfy me
the way it tasted on your lips

and that it's just the first month
of another year which exists
only to steal a little more of you
from my heart

ghostwriters

my life has become
little more than
a story penned
by ghostwriters
read aloud by strangers
with an ending
not mine to know

oxygen masks

I am deaf to the voice
over the loudspeaker
who says fit your own
oxygen mask
before helping others
and I wonder now
if that's why
I always fall
just shy of healing
I care too much
about everyone else
to ever save myself

falter

it calls to me
this precipice
of destruction
the void of despair
which crumbles
beneath bare feet
I falter in step
in faith, in hope
as I always do
because what good
comes from falling
except to realise
I've never had it in me
to fly

FALL

"There is freedom waiting for you, on the breezes of the sky. And you ask 'What if I fall?' Oh, but my darling, what if you fly?"

Erin Hanson

I am dying

they say everything blooms in spring
but I am dying

roots savagely ruptured
from the earth I call home

swagger of sunflowers
follow suit; bending, breaking

grassy blades
reclining, retreating

love in my heart
I can't stop it from fleeing
you don't see me bleeding

when I speak
you aren't heeding
instead say you are leaving
I pray I am dreaming

they say everything blooms in spring
they are lying
because me, I'm the only one dying

inner child

I am the grave within which
the ghost of my inner child
lies

abandoned spring

we gather
withering petals
of an abandoned spring
in our palms
look upon them
with compassion
as we attempt
to bring the beauty
of colour
into the cavern
of winter

but nothing
not even love
can breathe life
into a beautiful death

butterflies drowning

you fade as I hold you
breath lifting from your lungs
moonlight quivering in my chest

we are never destined to be
anything but butterflies drowning
in the rain

flickering flame

I burn still
a flickering flame
against your skin

do you know
even beautiful things
can hurt?

cracks in glass

I break quietly
cracks in a glass
you don't notice
until it shatters
until it is too late
to save me

midnight blankets

midnight blankets sing me lullabies
as dancing stars
speckled amid the loneliness
tease me with glimpses
of a happiness I once knew
still sleep will not come
I believe it has forsaken me
choosing to torment me
with all that I have lost
a delusion, a dream and memories
of what will never be

if you ask me how I am doing

I would tell you the kitchen bench
is covered in empty glasses
once half full
scattered between them
the crumbs of love you left me

I would tell you the blinds are down
and ring from your coffee cup
is now a permanent stain on my heart

maybe I could lie
and tell you I'm doing fine
that it doesn't hurt
as much as it used to
that I can breathe again
but we both know
the growing pile of sweaters
means I'm barely hanging on
to every tick of a clock long since dead

go on, ask me again how I'm doing
do as you do and cover your ears
when I reply
"I've never been more lost."

unravelling

in midnight hours, I unravel us
pulling at all the strands of love
you left me wrapped in
I replace them with webs
of loneliness; unworthiness
and worrying about the dawn
before it births
in case today, you walk away

tonight I'm burning it all
every kiss, every touch
every word that carefully
tiptoed into my heart
in readiness for goodbye

forget-me-nots

my wounds unfurl
like petals
aching to be loved
but you pluck them
like forget-me-nots
you love me
you love me
you love me
until you don't

uninhabitable

today, my body felt uninhabitable
as if there was more death
than life beneath my skin
until a tender waft of jasmine
took me back to your arms
to the sense of belonging
and safe harbour I knew
when you were mine

blindsided

I am blindsided
unsure how through
this tear-filled haze
I mistook the quiver
of your voice for fear
when all along
it was goodbye

trigger

the way it replays in my head
it's me who squeezes the trigger
blowing our dreams to hell

your headstone reads differently

graveyard

my heart is a graveyard
where headstones
all read the same

'love lived and died here
until she too
became nothing more
than a ghost'

lavender roses

I didn't even know
darkness had a name
until you trampled
life from the lavender roses
he planted in my heart
stripped me as bare
as autumn does the trees
and left me buried alive
in gun-metal grey

altar

you used my temple as an altar
pressed the cold metal barrel
as tightly as closed palms
against my skin
and pulled the trigger
but instead of a bullet
you filled my head with hate
clasped your hand tightly
over my mouth
and took away the only chance
I had, to beg you
to take aim and fire again
my death was always meant to be
both our answered prayers

grief knows my name

pink gerbera
blossom over
calcified bones

footprint shaped clouds
leave no hint
of heaven
for me to find

my heart
inherently blue
in memory
of the crispness
and inevitability
of a final breath

grief knows my name
and with it, I learn
there is no rest
in peace
enduring a death
that never ends

the last time I was angry
after @nik_poetry

the last time I was angry
I made a promise to God
maybe in the moment
I completely forgot I was a non-believer
I begged for his forgiveness, for mercy
for an end to this grief of losing you
I listened intently as the sky rumbled
with laughter so hard we both cried.
the truth is I wasn't angry at God
for taking you
I was angry he didn't take me too

I never saw him leaving

I can't bear the thought
your love might resemble his
I never saw him leaving
I only found him gone

shattered teardrops

there is no shame in shattered teardrops,
cleansing waters of sadness
escaping cliffs of lids in drips and drops,
wetting cheeks long ago kissed by lovers
in days when they framed the curl of a smile.
no there is no shame in shattered teardrops,
or in the cries of a heaving chest,
discarded and so immersed in pain
all that remains in their fractured reflections,
are reminders that we will never drown
no matter the deluge,
and that humans are stronger and braver
than in the moments before the tragedy
of a broken heart.

supposed to be

I wanted to kiss you
like it was the last time
feel your body against mine
like it was supposed to be
but you watched tears
stream down my face
told me you loved me
and left anyway

now I never want to hear
those words again

let me go

the only thing
more powerful
than the way
you held me
was how easily
you let me go

beauty in the flames

I am on fire
and you are
too busy
finding beauty
in the flames

stay

the greatest tragedy
of our love story was
you used your words
to hurt, not heal
your hands to crush
my wounded heart
and that you walked away
when all I ever needed
was for you to STAY

vulnerability

my demons
drew their swords
and laid them
at your feet
their vulnerability;
my first mistake

sharks

sharks infest these waters
baying for blood
and I am always easy prey
you make sure of that
every time you leave me
wounded and bleeding out

suicide pact

love never dies naturally
it is a murder/suicide pact
signed with three little words

I wonder if I will ever recover
from being loved by you

every now and then
I feel the weight of you
pressed into my bones,
see violet-tinged lips
once silenced by your hand
staring back at me,
you prised open my chest
as you did my thighs
and tore out my heart,
stealing from me,
everything I refused to give.
I wonder how you think
you left my mind untouched,
when my scars have healed
but everywhere I look
I see blood splattered onto sheets,
hear my own cries
reverberate these walls,
taste your betrayal on my lips
and I wonder,
if I will ever begin to recover
from being loved by you

godless child

my memories are twisted now
his reality versus mine
the tap of shoes on polished
floorboards spasm my spine
slow motion squeaking
of a rusted door-knob
reducing me to infancy
safe only in the cradle
of my own embrace
his husky growl
uncovering my barbie pink fairytales,
turning them to nightmares
recollections of a godless child's truth
and a gluttonous wolf's denial

Inspired by the quote You better not never tell nobody but God. - 'The Color Purple' By Alice Walker please don't tell me I'm not drowning

I was a child born of fire
dampened only by sea song
yet even I can't navigate this cataclysmic rip
and pull of life *(fire and water never mix)*
I was raised en pointe
but even that can't help my hesitance
to disturb the sand beneath my toes
(what if the ripple it causes pushes me under)
so what if I am on dry land
have you never heard of the phenomenon
of dry drowning
(I'm not being difficult, I am just making a point)
that death begins from the inside out,
*(no, my tears might not be the culprit but holding
them in might just begin my demise).*

so don't tell me I'm not drowning,
when I've been fighting for my life
right before your eyes
(why doesn't life come with a breathing apparatus)
sometimes no matter how you wave your arms,
lifeguards never come
*(remember it was you
who taught me to swim outside the flags)*
I'm flailing, falling, collapsing,
breaking, dying
(but no, according to you)
definitely not drowning

tattooed butterflies

you tattooed tiny butterflies on my ribs,
said it was the least you could do
after the trauma you had put me through
but their fluttering wings
made it hard to breathe,
maybe you knew they would,
maybe you knew all along
they would suffocate me
long after you were gone,
that's all love ever seems to do, after all.

words are poison

never trust twice
the person who believes
their words are poison
when they are proof
it is their silence
that kills

a shadow, a figment

I can't write
because pouring myself
onto the page
will leave me empty
then how will you
ever find me again
a shadow, a figment
of something
you could never manage
to choose

a list of things I did because
I wanted to be loved

I made myself small
hid in the shadows of a monster
learned silence was an ally
when words fell silent
I set fire to my dreams
watched smoke billow from the ruins
until it was thick enough
to choke air from my lungs
just the way your hands had
when blood stains
wallpapered the walls of my mind

bullet holes

you left me
riddled with bullet holes
knowing, it would
take only the tiniest crack
for sadness to creep through
instead you opened the door
let it devour me and left it
to call me home

blood on my hands

I didn't know
that I could
love too much
that my fingers
were clasped
too tightly
around the heart
you placed tenderly
in hollowed palms

I didn't know

I didn't know
this blood
on my hands
was yours

burning

for once
I didn't light
it all on fire

yet here I am
burning

dragging bones

I would have forgiven you
but here I am
dragging the bones
of apologies
which never
made a sound

leave me lonely

I am unsure why love
leaves me lonely
fractured moon
my only companion
a billion stars
with backs turned
darken in unison
perhaps it is that
you stole everything
that burned brightly
within me
so only by darkness
can I ever be found

these hands

I write poetry
with the lights off
so I do not have to face
my own words
they are the only things
I trust to these hands
which break everything
I have ever tried to love

into the distance

it scares me sometimes
that time has become
so thinly stretched
I can see far enough
into the distance
to see the end

casualty

we may just be
another casualty
of tragedy
turned poetry

scrub myself free

I bathe in the rain
for there is nothing more pure
than the tears of heaven
to scrub myself free of history

still innocence cannot wash
inscriptions from wrists
labels from skin
and scars from hearts
always destined to remain

broken compass

solitude has met me
with the fierceness
of a wild ocean
unpredictable swell
rising from depths unknown
crashing against
the hollows of my heart
I am rudderless and alone
with a broken compass
which knows of no place
called home

dead flowers

he tells me the dead flowers
I keep in my grandmothers
favourite vase remind him of me
I can't help but understand the metaphor,
wonder why he doesn't remember
it was he who plucked me
roots and all from
the warm embrace of Mother Earth
how when he trimmed me back
to bare stems
placed me in a glass house
to be worshipped
he never checked for cracks.
I have been starved of water
sunlight and love
and still, he fails to see
any fault in the stars of his eyes
which believe beauty is for the living
dying is beautiful too
or at least it could be
if it wasn't me he failed
to see with petals falling at my feet

pale blue sundress

my pain is a pale blue sundress
imitating the reflection of my eyes
you tell me they captivate you
are the reason you stay
as if I needed another excuse
not to heal

these trembling hands

these trembling hands
have become judge,
jury and executioner
they have betrayed me
time and time again
held me here against my will
let go of everything I hold dear
I guess what I am trying to say is
they are as weak as I am
as broken as I am
as lost as I am
and still, they hold on
why, is what I'm still trying
to understand

surrender

here is my surrender
beneath the weight
of a world I never
really belonged to
bury me with fondness
with kindness
with all of the love
I gave but never received
smile and remember
me always
here is my surrender

fear is

fear is the lingering nagging
in the back of my mind
a deep-seated dread
that any second
that phone will ring
everything will go black
and I will be transported
back to the misery
back to that broken;
long-forgotten me
who took too many years
to try and piece herself
back together and even then;
never truly did

parched well

I yearn to be more
than a parched well
in an arid desert
awaiting rains
which never come
to fill my empty cup
with more than a mirage
of sparkling waters
of love which long ago
died of thirst

trample me softly

if you must
trample me softly
do not scar me
with the weight of love
or leave faded imprints
of promises you made
as you turn and walk away
instead lie as you kiss me
I am getting used to
collecting goodbyes

beauty in blades

the darkness has your smile
it kisses the nape of my neck
as it whispers
'even diamonds become
beautiful when cut'
so I draw you in blades
across my skin
bleed for the cause, for my life
for the chance to once again
be beautiful to anyone but you

FLY

"Hold fast to dreams, for if dreams die,
Life is a broken-winged bird that cannot fly."

Langston Hughes

brim full

I am brim full
of apologies
a balancing
act on the
hollowed edges
of almost
and I am
not looking
back, because
for all that
I am not
I am still more
than you deserve

crimson blood of held tongues

I pen letters to ghosts
sacred messages
in crimson blood
of held tongues
smudge words with tears
of apologies never uttered
no longer imperative
to healing
I burn along with them
trauma in flames
turns to scattered ashes
spawning a phoenix
ascending the afterglow

bow down, demons
watch her rise

I call them poetry

I thought I kept
my wounds hidden
but for years
I have let them
bleed onto pages
and called them
poetry

ancient cradle

this numbness
has become home
an ancient cradle
soothing my
wounded heart

what I mean to say is
I'm glad I didn't
feel you leave

mistaking a season for forever

the winter brings us back
to bare bones
warmth peeling easily from our skin
without sun to thaw us
and we mistake a season
for forever
when it was only ever meant
for the longing of another's arms

purple pansies

it's 3pm
and the blinds are down
cracks of light
paint shadow puppets
on my skin
as the warmth swims by
searching for a destination
to settle and stay
it picks purple pansies
who lean into the light
and bow cordially
smiling back
in all their open petal glory
and I smile too
because amid the darkness
their mid-afternoon rendezvous
takes me back to loving you

hellbent

these seasons keep changing
but here I am, still the same
hellbent on loving you

trembling blades of grass

I tuck my tears
between trembling
blades of grass
a safekeeping of hope
that one day
something beautiful
may grow
from all this pain

I fell in love

I fell in love with his touch
before I ever felt his hands
with his smile
before I ever memorised it
with the love in his words
before I ever heard his voice
the truth is
I fell in love with him
long before we met

where love goes to die

I am consumed
by the empty grave
embedded in my chest
this lonely place
where love goes to die

promise me
we will be different
this time…

my hand is yours

I had forgotten
the way my hand fit yours
how it enveloped all of me completely
and I'm not sure I like it anymore
this overwhelming fear
sitting in the base of my throat
the inevitable, hiding
in creases of your palms
because I have known
the leaving of your fingertips
one too many times to feel safe
and yet here I am; holding on
this time willing myself to stay

still beating

promise me
the battle is worth it
that these bruises
are not just for show
and this heart
ripped, still beating
from my chest
is enough for you
to love

aligning stars

it was not
the aligning
of stars
he said
for us
it was
our scars

afraid to make sense

don't be afraid to say yes
to open your heart
and let love in
but always remember
your heart is your own
no one can break anything
you are not willing to give

anchor

hold me close
like the warm breeze
of a Sunday afternoon
let your chest be a place
to anchor my dreams
your lips safe harbour
for my secrets
and your heart
the only place to belong

evening dress of shadows

I am still
beneath a
blue moon
adorned in an
evening dress
of shadows
feeling at home
with one foot in
and the other
just shy of heaven
a hop, skip, and jump
from your arms

retracing steps

let us retrace our steps
back to where
we abandoned our hearts
but this time
why don't we stay?

quiver

the way petals tremble
beneath a drop of rain
reminds me of you
frigid winter morns
and soft lips
against closed lids
teasing light from dark
until we quiver at will
beneath the sway
of love

canopy of scars

my body wears a canopy of scars
destitute words in cursive shades
of dormant ink
revealing a tormented fragility
awkwardly disguised with a smile
and an eagerness to alter
a lifetime of narcissistic narratives
beneath the delicacy of his touch

molten skies

I remember you
at twilight
molten skies
cascading o'er
pearlescent skin
rapturous dusk
clutching at the
rising warmth
of blushed cheeks
every inch of me
keeper of your touch
a faint collection
of butterfly kisses
enduring vestiges
of love

summer days

your touch on my skin, lingers
the way drawn out summer days
birth mellow sunsets
our silhouette suspended
dancing contours onto these sheets
but your warmth
has long since faded
swallowed by these valleys
of solitude
and I yearn
oh how I yearn
to unearth paradise
once more with you

storytellers

his eyes are storytellers
and I am a ship
lost at sea
in their words

barefoot

fragments of the woman I was
embedded themselves
into your sole
when you walked
barefoot into my life

sometimes you would sit
cross-legged
tweezers in hand
pulling bloody slivers
of me from your skin

you told me
even when it hurt
you would carry me
through it all

true to your word
despite the agony
of loving me
you never once
asked for shoes

reflection and window

love is both a reflection
and a window
until we can accept
the person looking back
we cannot do justice
to the hearts of those looking in

read my thoughts

I wonder if he can read my mind
filled with pages of unwritten poetry
desperate to be inked
between beats of his heart
as he dreams

makeshift love letter

consider my ashes
a makeshift love letter
an inscription upon
the hollowness of time
read it with soft hands
and a kind heart
with my name now
tattooed on your bones

almost

if ever
there was
a definition
of almost
it surely
must
be us

stark naked

poets' hearts dance
stark naked
on a page
to the cadence
we call poetry

you don't read my poetry anymore

so I must update you:
I still love you, I'm sure you know that
I am not strong enough to say goodbye,
don't get me wrong, I am moving on
but I just can't leave your ghost alone
on the cold concrete of the past.
our song topped my most played list
this year but I never let anyone hear it
because it is the last part of you
that I don't have to share.
your roses have blossomed
but my heart has not
it's too soon, too hard,
too unfathomable to believe that
this eternal graveyard
is love's home now.

I am yet to find peace or happiness
yet but I only hope that you have.

in another reality

in another reality the sun rises
and sets in your eyes
instead of through my tears
the warmth of my hands
comes from the softness of yours
not my morning cup of tea
the voices in my head are mine
and not you wishing me harm
the ocean is a sweep of blue
instead of my heart
lyrics don't act as knives
gauging at my still-beating heart
and this poem is written
by a stranger in another time
because I am yours and you are mine

teach me

teach me how to be beautiful
the kind deserving of love

show me my softness
so I can use it
to file away the splinters
which keep your loving arms
at bay

help me embrace the silence
you see as the enemy
when is in fact, safety and home

prove to me that I am enough
as I was, as I am
and as I will always be

if you are looking for me, you'll find me

dipping toes in tepid blues
of a sun-kissed ocean for when I'm lost
I always find myself tucked
'tween ebb and flow.

clinging to pappi of dandelions
a wafting breeze
carrying me to infinite freedom

soul deep in a book filled with poetry, vicariously
living a life I cannot.

hands wrapped tightly
round a warm mug of memories
as embers of love smoulder
in a firepot at my feet.

here on a page
where I will remain
long after I am but a memory
outliving the hearts of the ones I love.

bury me

do not love me when I am gone
or read poetry atop my grave
let your mouth savour everything unsaid
until you are parched of words
do not write me eulogies
but pen me love letters
that I can read repeatedly
do not entomb me
with everything important to you
love me enough
to bury me with pockets full of love

my psychologist told me I have an addictive
personality

so I gave up living
tried to limit my exposure
to antidepressants and love
but who was I kidding
I craved the high of your lips

I tried building walls
became addicted to them too
I felt safer in the confines of loneliness
than I ever did with my heart on my sleeve, exposed
and bruised

I attempted smaller portions
I let love chase me then chose goodbye
all that got me was a reputation
and a heart like a revolving door

I tried hypnotherapy
but when they asked me to visualise home
I found myself in the depths of your eyes
and the safety of your arms, again and again

my psychologist told me
I have an addictive personality
I told her I'm ok with that
I mean, I can think of plenty of worse ways
to die

the person I used to be

if one day
you leave flowers
upon my grave
leave them only
for the person
I used to be

he has your eyes

he has your eyes
the infancy
of crinkled lines
showing a lifetime
of laughter
oh yes he has your eyes
by which I mean
I never thought another
would see as deeply
into my soul as you did

our story

I have committed
our story
to memory
now I immortalise
its beauty
in words

falling in love with autumn

each love lost
is like leaves
loosening grasp
of branches
collecting in piles
waiting to be the reason
someone falls in love
with autumn

things I learned in 2023

even shattered things can be beautiful
after fragments of light break through
the sun is brave and persistent
it continues to rise despite everything
something I am yet to learn how to do

love is a state of mind
when I can't love myself
no one else can either
the road less travelled is now crowded
I can no longer find peace here

I cried more than I laughed
lost more than I found
broke more than I healed and that's ok

words were my best friend
it was heartbreaking
to be abandoned by them too

life is too short, too fleeting
gone in the blink of an eye
and I will be too
before I can put into practice
all the things I have learned.

just a girl

I'm just a girl
wading through
neck-deep darkness
begging you
to find softness
in my heart
and protect it
as your own
before the ugliness
of this world
swallows it whole
and I become
a veil
of who I am meant to be

simplicity

I have always adored simplicity
stripped-back nakedness
of body, mind and soul
the kind which comes from
familiarity, acceptance
and falling in love
with yourself

earth after rain

loneliness
is wondering
if it is only I
who falls in love
with the smell
of the earth after rain

bereft

my window sits still
open to the possibility
of apricot sunsets
and cobalt blues
footprints collect
here on the sill
of blue fairy wren
and glass butterflies
but I wonder why
when I open my heart
the same way
exquisite beauty
always finds me here
bereft, breathless
waiting for more

imposter

I am lowercase letters
disguised metaphors
undotted i's
uncrossed t's
grammatical errors
broken stanzas
and offbeat rhymes
an imposter of poetry
bleeding words
hoping you will
read them anyway

do not fall in love with people like me

people like me
who are the children of carpenters
born with pre-existing walls
built in preparation for the trauma

people like me
who don't learn lessons easily
who forgive the unforgivable
but hold tightly to ghosts
of the little things you did or did not say

people like me
who are afraid of being abandoned
so we will run before you have the chance

people like me
who write the words 'I love you'
at the end of every text
but delete them because we are too afraid
of the weight of our words.

people like me
who long to be held
but are afraid to be touched

people like me
who use the word fine
but don't know the meaning
except that it always brings an end
to your questions.

people like me
who write poetry
about reasons not to love
people like me

keepers

I am covered in scars
by which I mean
they are the keepers
of unwritten poetry
no one will ever read

edge of light

I teeter at the edge of light
where seasons turn
dusk clutching
tree canopies
desperate for just
one more moment
I question why exist
amid such beauty
and why it illuminates
every living being
but me

unblur the lines

each breath traverses in a hum
a question, hanging in the air
bitter taste of last nights
whiskey regret
poisoning my tongue
until it is numb, like me
without the pain

I seek out the gentle caress
of dawn, gone are the string
of the blinding summer sun
on a repeat of yesterday
yawn, loud enough
to rattle bruised ribs
but not enough to wake
a sleeping world
yet none of me is tired

I smile with eyes
that have known home
as sombre thoughts
I am yet to find an escape from
but am no longer consumed by

I feel everything
try to learn the word felt
so as to unblur the lines
between then and now
past and present
broken and whole
to save myself

each breath traverses in a hum
a question, hanging in the air
it is not pain, but life
now settling in my soul

toothpick bones

I can't change
so the seasons do

coaxing growth
from these
flesh covered
toothpick bones

there might just
be hope for me yet

fledgling

no one can stop
the female fledgling
trusting strength of wing
to the power of flight
absolute in her ability
to soar

ABOUT THE AUTHOR

Karen Richards resides in Tasmania, Australia. She is a writer of poetry and prose, and the author of three poetry collections: Release the Fireflies, Wrapped in Folds of Midnight and The Way My Words Fall all of which are available on Amazon and in all good book stores online.

Karen has been writing poetry for over 35 years and enjoys connecting with her audience with emotion and simplicity through shared experiences.

Karen has shared her work through numerous publishing opportunities in zines and anthologies including Unite Zine raising money for the Peter Mac Cancer Centre, Silver City Anthology, Red Penguin, Riveting Rants, Poetic Reveries and the Poetry in Motion Project.

Karen currently writes to a social media audience, and her works can be found on Instagram, Threads, and X.